T0182436

Ode to Grapefruit

How JAMES EARL JONES Found His Voice

Kari Lavelle

Illustrated by
Bryan Collier

Alfred A. Knopf  New York

Please skip my turn, Mrs. Gardiner.

Not me.

Please.

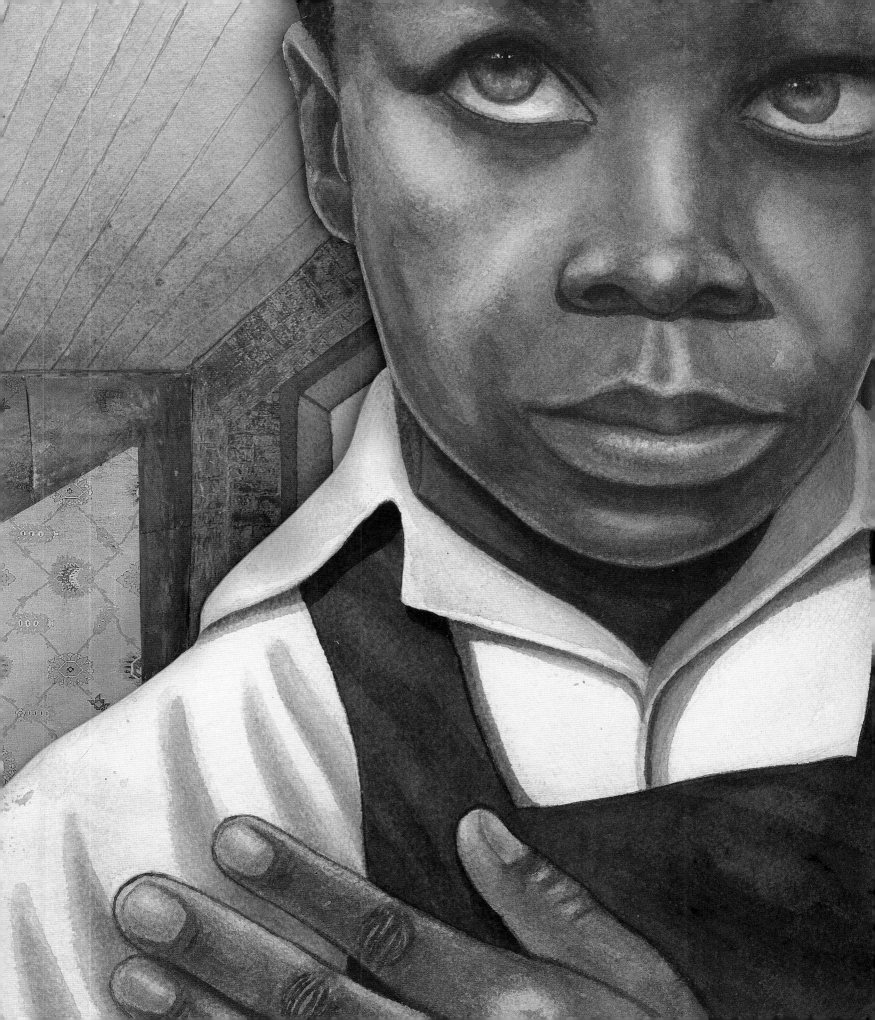

But it was his turn to read.
James stood up—
    reluctantly.
He *knew* those words on the page.
Silence surrounded him,
    all eyes waiting, watching.

He remembered the last time he read aloud.
Face burning.
Heart racing.
Kids laughing.
Mouth trying.
Voice blocking.

James thumped back down in his seat.

Why do my words get stuck when I need them the most?

James escaped to his special place,
the wall behind the hay barn.
Back at home,
his words flowed.

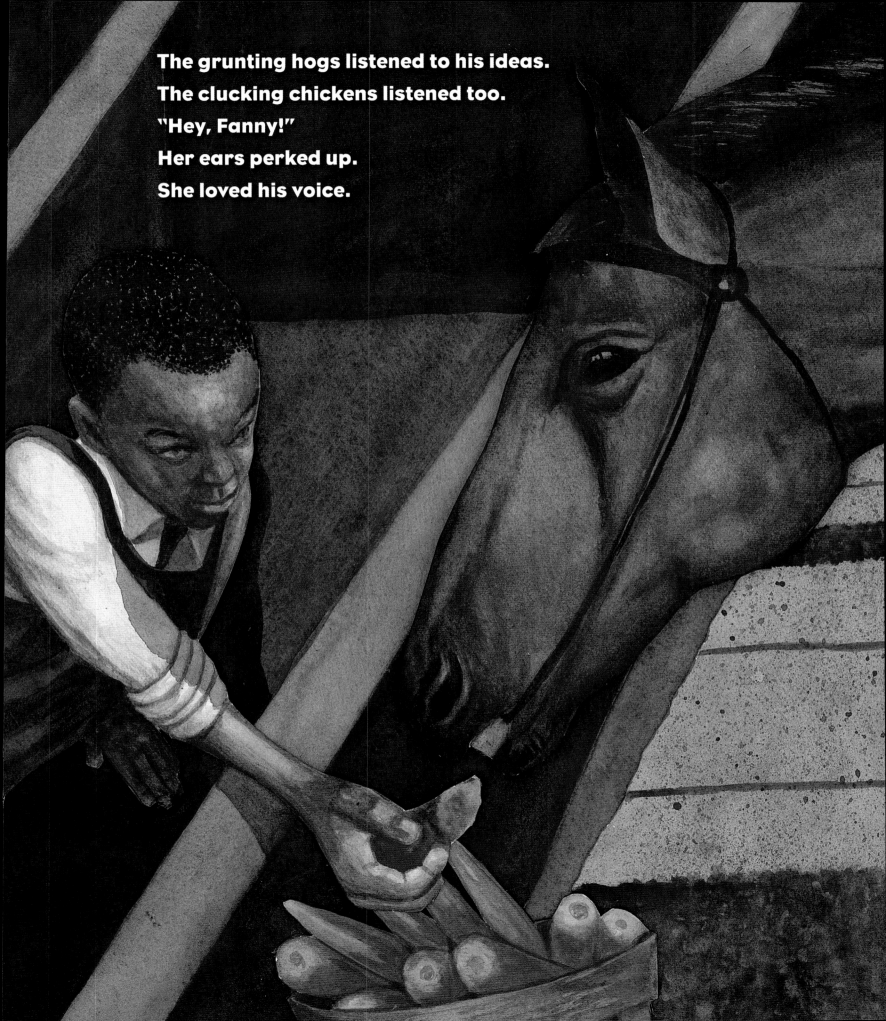

The grunting hogs listened to his ideas.
The clucking chickens listened too.
"Hey, Fanny!"
Her ears perked up.
She loved his voice.

James grew,
　　his stuttering stayed.
"This is James Earl," Papa said
　　when a visitor arrived.
James opened his mouth.
But his jaw tensed.
His throat tightened.
His voice, trapped.
No sound.

"James, say hello," Mama urged.
I'm trying.
He pounded his feet.
He gritted his teeth—
　　to force the words out.
But it didn't work.
So he just nodded.

James was done talking.
He would stay silent.
No more asking questions.
No more sharing ideas.
His emotions stuck inside.
If he didn't talk,
    he wouldn't stutter.
So James listened.

He listened to the news.
He listened to Aunt Willeva's songs
    and Uncle H.B.'s fingers striking the piano keys.
He listened to Mama's words, planting seeds of stories for his dreams.

At school,
James listened
and James learned.
He wrote answers for teachers.
He nodded to friends.

Off to high school.
New building and new teachers—
like Professor Crouch,
who loved poetry.

His teacher recited poems aloud.
James loved listening to the rhythm
and the words.
Professor Crouch wanted the students
    to memorize poems.
"If you love poetry,
    you've got to be able to say it out loud.
    That's what poetry is."

Say it out loud?
No way!

But when he was alone,
James found his voice reciting
the irresistible patterns of poetry.

"By the shores of Gitche Gumee,
By the shining Big-Sea-Water."
Poetry presented a new way
for James to express himself.
He penned his own poems—
in secret.

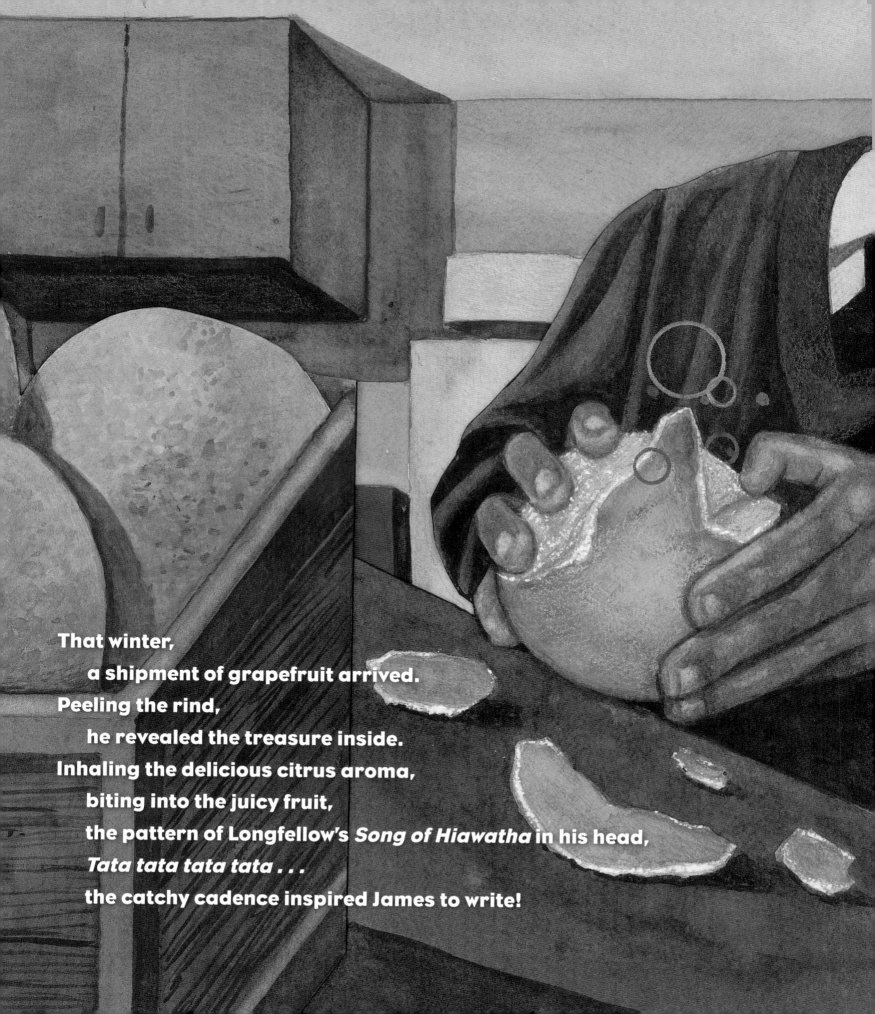

That winter,
   a shipment of grapefruit arrived.
Peeling the rind,
   he revealed the treasure inside.
Inhaling the delicious citrus aroma,
   biting into the juicy fruit,
   the pattern of Longfellow's *Song of Hiawatha* in his head,
Tata tata tata tata . . .
   the catchy cadence inspired James to write!

James gave his poem to Professor Crouch.
"This is a fine poem. Did you copy it?"
James shook his head *no*.
"The best way for you to demonstrate that
you wrote this poem yourself is for you
to say it aloud to the class."

James stood up,

for himself.

He traveled to the front of the classroom,
the dark side of fear rising.
Heart pounding.
Eighteen sets of eyes
and Professor Crouch watching.
Some kids smirked and some smiled.
Knees shaking.

But he felt the rhythm in his soul.
Tata tata tata tata . . .
James opened his mouth and began,
his voice deep and smooth,
reciting from his heart,
"Ode to Grapefruit . . ."

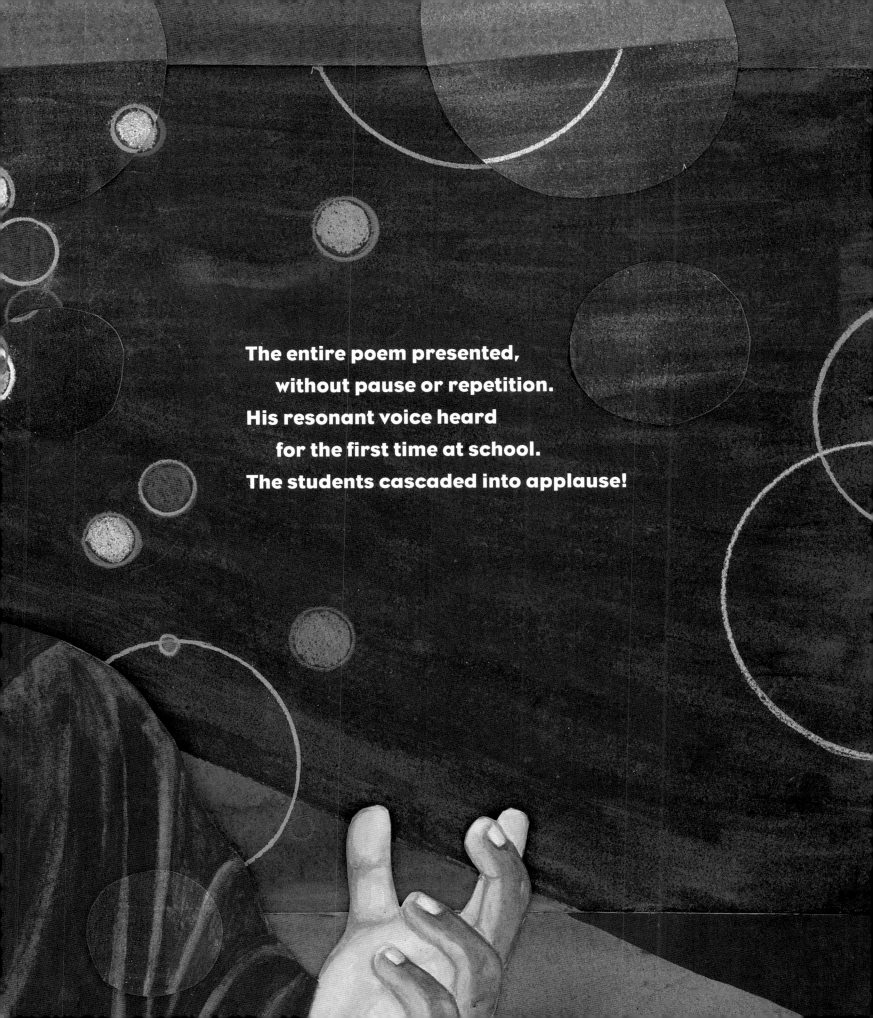

The entire poem presented,
    without pause or repetition.
His resonant voice heard
    for the first time at school.
The students cascaded into applause!

In poetry and literature, James found his voice.
He performed Chaucer for others—
"If gold rusts, what then can iron do?"

He read Shakespeare to the animals—
"Not marble nor the gilded monuments
of princes shall outlive this powerful rhyme . . ."

He recited Edgar Allan Poe on stage—
"Once upon a m-m-midnight dreary . . ."
James still stuttered at times.

But he knew his voice was important.
Imperfectly perfect.

James debated and acted,
    won a public speaking championship,
    and earned a college scholarship!
Now people listened—
    to his questions,
    to his ideas,
    to his emotions.

After eight years of silence,
James found his voice,
 low and booming,
  beyond the dark side of fear.

With patience and practice,
 the legendary sound
 of James Earl Jones
 would soon be known
 around the world.

Author's Note

Nothing can bring you peace but yourself.
Nothing can bring you peace but the triumph of principles.
—Ralph Waldo Emerson, "Self-Reliance"

James Earl Jones was born in Arkabutla, Mississippi, on January 17, 1931. This story begins when James is five, right after he moved away from his mother, joining his grandparents, aunts, and uncles in Michigan. James's mother stayed in Mississippi, and he was raised by his maternal grandparents, "Mama" and "Papa." Though James was surrounded by love, it was difficult for him to be away from his mother. He also lived with a lot of extended family, including his uncle Randy, who was only four years older and more like a brother to James.

When James was around ten years old, Randy had a seizure. James raced through a blizzard to get to the general store. He tried to tell Mr. Fortelka, the store owner, to call a doctor, but his words kept blocking when he tried to speak. Eventually, James communicated his message, and the doctor was called. The doctor arrived to help Randy just in time, but the shame James felt about his stuttering remained with him for years.

In his autobiography, *Voices and Silences*, Mr. Jones shared several of his experiences with racial injustice. When eleven-year-old James heard the news that an anti-lynching bill had failed in Congress, he was enraged. One of his aunts handed him a pen and paper. He poured all of his anger into his writing. Just 169 words later, James sent the letter to the editor of the *Grand Rapids Herald*, where it was published with the title "Coals of Fire upon Heads of Whites." For the first time, he felt like his words mattered.

After a regional forensics and debate meet in Traverse City, Michigan, Professor Donald Crouch took James out to dinner at a fancy restaurant. When the whites-only establishment refused to serve James, they had to find somewhere else to eat. The elation James felt from his performance that day was instantly crushed by the unjust constraints of his country.

James Earl Jones credits Professor Crouch, the teacher who had previously worked with the famous poet Robert Frost, as "the father of my resurrected voice." On the last day of high school, James received a gift from Professor Crouch—a copy of Ralph Waldo Emerson's "Self-Reliance." James stayed in contact with Professor Crouch long after his graduation.

After high school, James Earl Jones went on to attend the University of Michigan. He has since starred in numerous plays, television shows, and movies during his almost-seventy-year acting career. He has won three Tony Awards, two Emmy Awards, a Golden Globe, and a Grammy. James Earl Jones was given an honorary Academy Award and a Lifetime Achievement Tony Award. In 2022, the Cort Theatre, in Manhattan's fabled Theater District, was renamed the James Earl Jones Theatre. He provided the voices for many productions, including Mufasa in *The Lion King* and Darth Vader in the Star Wars series. Mr. Jones's iconic voice is valued worldwide for its deep resonance, yet many do not realize he has always considered himself a stutterer. "I don't say I was 'cured.' I'm still a stutterer. I just work with it," he said.

This narrative attempted to stay as close to the facts as possible. All dialogue (Professor Crouch, Mama, Papa) comes directly from Mr. Jones's accounts of the events. The limited dialogue from James was invented; it felt essential to have James speak both fluently ("Hey, Fanny!") and disfluently ("Once upon a m-m-midnight dreary . . .") in a book about stuttering. There were no accounts of specific stuttered responses; however, Mr. Jones shared experiences of blocks (no sound) and expressed that words containing an *m* were particularly difficult. Some of the descriptions of Mr. Jones's stutters were based on my experience working with other people who stutter.

Mr. Jones's story is a lesson for all of us in acceptance and listening to the voice within us. We all can transform—just as James Earl Jones did, exiting his eight years of silence to become one of the most beloved and recognizable voices in the world.

As a speech pathologist for over fifteen years, I continue to share the inspirational story of James Earl Jones with many kids who stutter. In researching and then writing his story, it is my hope his voice gives a voice to many.

—*Kari Lavelle*

Illustrator's Note

The story of young James Earl Jones is one of determination and finding his inner voice. Early on in life, as an African American boy, James faced many obstacles, such as systemic racism and classism, in addition to his stutter. This book shares some of his journey from intense struggle to the bright lights of success. The art was created using watercolor and collage, and in certain areas, you will notice circles or bubbles. These indicate both the presence of music and when James is in a dreamlike state, visually heightening and further expressing James's inner emotions. I wanted to show how the discovery of the musicality in language is the key that opens up a doorway to a wonder world: a safe place where James found his voice. James Earl Jones is living proof that through hard work and perseverance, each of us can find our triumphant voice—and change the world.

—*Bryan Collier*

About Stuttering

What is stuttering?

Stuttering (or stammering) is a communication disorder in which speech is characterized by sound prolongations (sssss-stutter), repetitions (stut-stut-stutter), or blocks (no sound).

What should I do if I'm talking to someone who stutters?

Be kind. Be patient. Listen to their message. Don't try to offer word suggestions if they get stuck.

How many people stutter?

About one percent of the world's population stutters. And about five percent of children stutter at some point in their development. Stuttering resolves for about eighty percent of these children.

Is there a cure for stuttering?

There are no miracle cures for stuttering. But there are many ways to help people who stutter. Poetry, debate, and acting helped James Earl Jones gain confidence in his communication. Speech pathologists can also help people who stutter. An important thing to know is that people who stutter can do the same jobs as people who don't stutter.

For more information on stuttering, please visit:

stutteringhelp.org

blankcenterforstuttering.org

Selected Sources

Ackroyd, Peter, and Geoffrey Chaucer. *The Canterbury Tales: A Retelling.* London: Penguin Classics, 2009.

Cuomo, Matilda Raffa. *The Person Who Changed My Life: Prominent People Recall Their Mentors.* Emmaus, PA: Rodale Books, 2011.

Emerson, Ralph Waldo. *Self-Reliance and Other Essays.* Mineola, NY: Dover Publications, 2012.

Hajek, Danny. "James Earl Jones: From Stutterer to Janitor to Broadway Star." *All Things Considered,* NPR, November 9, 2014.

Jones, James Earl. "James Earl Jones on the Importance of Mentoring." *Guideposts,* June 12, 2017.

Jones, James Earl, and Penelope Niven. *Voices and Silences.* New York: Charles Scribner's Sons, 1993.

The Lion King. Dir. Roger Allers and Rob Minkoff. Walt Disney Studios, 1994. Film.

Longfellow, Henry Wadsworth. *The Song of Hiawatha.* New York: Dutton, 1960.

Poe, Edgar Allan. "The Raven." *Edgar Allan Poe: Complete Tales and Poems.* Edison, NJ: Castle Books, 2002.

The Sandlot. Dir. David Mickey Evans. Island World/20th Century Fox, 1993. Film.

Shakespeare, William. *Love Poems and Sonnets of William Shakespeare.* New York: Doubleday, 1991.

Star Wars: Episode VI: Return of the Jedi. Dir. Richard Marquand. 20th Century Fox, 1983. Film.

For anyone discovering their voice—
and to those who helped me find mine.

—Kari Lavelle

I want to give special thanks and dedication to
Mrs. DeMarco and her class at Marlboro Elementary
School for their participation as models for this project.

—Bryan Collier

THIS IS A BORZOI BOOK PUBLISHED BY ALFRED A. KNOPF

Text copyright © 2024 by Kari Lavelle
Illustrations copyright © 2024 by Bryan Collier

All rights reserved. Published in the United States by Alfred A. Knopf,
an imprint of Random House Children's Books, a division of Penguin Random House LLC, New York.

Knopf, Borzoi Books, and the colophon are registered trademarks of Penguin Random House LLC.
Visit us on the Web! rhcbooks.com
Educators and librarians, for a variety of teaching tools, visit us at RHTeachersLibrarians.com

Library of Congress Cataloging-in-Publication Data is available upon request.
ISBN 978-0-593-37276-0 (trade) — ISBN 978-0-593-37277-7 (lib. bdg.) — ISBN 978-0-593-37278-4 (ebook)

The text of this book is set in 16-point Eagle Book.
The illustrations were created using watercolor and collage.

Editor: Rotem Moscovich
Designer: Martha M. Rago
Copy Editor: Artie Bennett
Managing Editor: Jake Eldred
Production Manager: Melissa Fariello

MANUFACTURED IN CHINA
10 9 8 7 6 5 4 3 2 1
First Edition

Random House Children's Books supports the First Amendment and celebrates the right to read.

"Look, Simba. Everything the light touches is our kingdom."

—James Earl Jones as
Mufasa in *The Lion King*

"Baseball was life!
And I was good at it . . .
real good."

—James Earl Jones as
Mr. Mertle in *The Sandlot*